Nancy Lindop's Genealogies
Volume 2

Hampton and Grindley

By
Nancy and Geoffrey Lindop

First published 2014
Revised 2015

Published by:
Mercianotes
Wigton
CA7 5AQ
United Kingdom

http://www.mercianotes.com

© 2015 Mercianotes

Follow the latest titles / updates
on Twitter @Mercianotes

ISBN: 978-1-905999-22-4

Contents

The Hamptons of Mucklestone

First published 2008 by Mercianotes as a separate booklet
under ISBN: 978-1-905999-08-8

The Hampton Family in Shropshire

First published 2015 by Mercianotes as part of this publication
under ISBN: 978-1-905999-22-4

The Grindley Family Of North Shropshire

First published 2009 by Mercianotes as a separate booklet
under ISBN: 9781-905999-12-5

The Hamptons of Mucklestone

Alice Alyce Allys Alls

49D01 Alyce Hampton
  Buried 20 February 1564

49D02 Alls Hampton
  Buried 27 March 1564

56B01 Allys Hampton
  Daughter of Henry (54M01) and Jone (54M01)
  Baptised 20 April 1568

59B01 Alls Hampton
  Daughter of Robert (57M02) and Anne (57M01) of
  Wetherington
  Baptised 28 September 1599

Amy Amey

56M01 Amey Hampton
  Wife of Robert Hampton (56B01)
  Born Amey Fox
  Married Robert Hampton 8 January 1589
  Married John Mason 20 November 1603

57M01 Amy Hampton
  1st Wife of John Hampton (57M01)
  Born Amy Meridith
  Married John Hampton 28 January 1590
  Children:
        59B03 John
  Hanged herself 14 July 1601

Ann, Anne, An Ane

54D01 Anne Hampton
  Wife of William Hampton (59M02?)
  Buried 17 December 1617
  - see An (59B02)

57M01   Anne Hampton
    Wife of Robert Hampton (57M01)
    Children:
          59B01 Thomas
          59B01 John
          59B01An
          59B01Alls

59B01 An Hampton
    Daughter of Robert (57M01) and Anne (57M01)
    Baptised 12 September 1595

59M02 An Hampton
    Wife of William Hampton (59M02)
    Born An Roe. She was from Mucklestone when she married, but
    no record of her being born there.
    Married William 2 August 1610
    Possibly Buried 17 December 1617 - see Anne (54D01)

59M03 An Hampton
    Wife of Hughe Hampton (59M01)
    Children:
          61B01 An
    Buried 10 November 1637

61B01 An Hampton
    Daughter of Hughe Hampton (59M01) and An (59M03)
    Baptised 7 November 1610

62M01 Anne Hampton
    Wife of William Hampton (62M01)
    Children:
          64B02 Katherne

Edmund

49D01 Edmund Hampton
    Buried 3 February 1563

Ellen

53M01 Ellen Hampton
    Wife of William (53M01)
    Born Ellen Moss
    Married William Hampton 10 October 1556
    Children:
            56B01 Robert

56B01 Ellen Hampton
    Daughter of Henry (54M01) and Jone (54M01)
    Baptised 26 July 1562

59B01 Ellen Hampton
    Daughter of Hugh Hampton (56M02)
            and Jaine Wetherington (56M01)
    Baptised 26 November 1595

59B02 Ellen Hampton
    Daughter of John (57M03) and Elizabeth (57M01)
    Baptised 21 August 1599

Ellinor Elnor

56B01 Elnor Hampton
    Daughter of John (53M01) and Margeret (53M01)
    Baptised 4 March 1566

Elizabeth

56M01 Elizabeth Hampton
    Wife of John Hampton (56M02)
    Born Elizabeth Hasaldine
    Married John Hampton 15 June 1584
    Children:
            58B01 John
    Buried 25 January 1591

57M01 Elizabeth Hampton
Wife of John Hampton (57M03)
Maiden name unknown. She lived in Wethington (Winnington)
Children:
59B01 Nicholas
59B02 Ellen

60M01 Elizabeth Hampton
Wife of Thomas Hampton (60B01)
Born Elizabeth Trym
Married Thomas 5 August 1621
Children:
62B01 Mary

She probably died between 18 September 1625 and 25 March 1631.
The pages of the parish register are missing for this period and by
September 1631 Thomas had married Mary and had a son by her.

61B01 Elizabeth Hampton
Daughter of John (59M05) and Gracie (59M01)
Baptised 31 August 1623

Frances

57M01 Frances Hampton
Wife of William Hampton (57M01)
Born Frances Bryst
Married William Hampton 6 May 1590
Died at Blower Dales, Blore
Buried 1 July 1610

Francis

53D01 Francis Hampton
Brother of Hughe Hampton of Dorrington.
Buried 13 October 1603

He could be Francis (55B01) in which case his brother is not
recorded. Or he could be the brother of Hughe (53M01), in which
case when was he born and who was his father? A similar argument
applies to Hugh (59M01) and Hugh (56M02).

55B01 Francis Hampton
　　　Son of Hughe (53M01) and Margerie (53M01)
　　　Baptised 15 January 1555
　　　Possibly buried 13 October 1603 - see 53D01

Gracie

59M01 Gracie Hampton
　　　Wife of John Hampton (59M05)
　　　Children:
　　　　　　61B01 Lawrence
　　　　　　61B01 Elizabeth

Henry

54M01 Henry Hampton
　　　Married Jone (54M01)
　　　Children:
　　　　　　56B01 Ellen
　　　　　　56B01 Hughe
　　　　　　56B01 Allys
　　　　　　57B01 Jone

Hugh Hughe

52C01 Hugh Hampton
　　　Hanged himself on 9 May 1571

53M01 Hughe Hampton
　　　Married Margerie (53M01)
　　　Children:
　　　　　　Francis 55B01

56B01 Hughe Hampton
　　　Son of Henry (54M01) and Jone (54M02)
　　　Baptised 7 March 1564

56M02 Hugh Hampton
Married Jaine Wetherington (56M01) 4 December 1585
Children:
        58B01 Margaret
        59B01 Jaine
        59B01 Richard
        59B01 Ellen
        59B02 John
        60B01 Thomas
        60B01 William

59M01 Hughe Hampton
Married An (59M03)
Children:
        61B01 An

63B01 Hugh Hampton
Son of Richard (61M01) and Margery (61M01)
Baptised 20 January 1632

Jane Jaine

56M01 Jaine Hampton
Wife of Hugh Hampton (56M02)
Born Jaine Wetherington
Married Hugh Hampton 4 December 1585
Children:
        58B01 Margaret
        59B01 Jaine
        59B01 Richard
        59B01 Ellen
        59B02 John
        60B01 Thomas
        60B80 William

59B01 Jaine Hampton
Daughter of Hugh Hampton (56M02)
        and Jaine Wetherington (56M01)
Baptised 4 August August 1590

John

49D01 John Hampton
   Buried 29 December 1565

52D01 John Hampton of Carnecot
   Buried 20 September 1576

53M01 John Hampton
   Married Margeret Cranadg (53M01) 28 October 1556
   Children:
               55B01 Margeriet
               56B01 John
               56B01 Elnor
               56B01 Katherine
               57B01 Rondolphe
   Buried 4 May 1596†

54D01 John Hampton
   Son of Hughe
   Buried 17 April 1616††

54D02 John Hampton
   A servant
   Buried 7 February 1619 ††

55D01 John Hampton
   Buried 2 October 1624 ††

56B01 John Hampton
   Son of John (53M01) and Margeret (53M01)
   Baptised 24 February 1563
   Buried 4 May 1596
56M02 John Hampton
   Possibly the same as 56B01
   Married Elizabeth Hasaldine (56M01) 15 June 1584
   Children:
               58B01 John

57M01 John Hampton
   Married (1) Amy Meridith (57M01) 28 January 1590
   Children:
                 59B03   John
                 59B01   Margeret?
                 59B01   Raphe?

   Married (2) Katherin Harper (64M01) 23 September 1602
   It is unlikely that the children with question marks were part of
   this family.

57M02   John Hampton
   Married Margerie Wethington (57M01) 20 November 1592
   Children:
                 59B01   Margeret?
                 59B04   John
                 59B01   William
                 59B01   Raphe?
   It is very likely that the children with question marks were part of
   this family.

57M03 John Hampton
   Married Elizabeth (57M02) of Wethington (or Winnington)
   Children:
                 59B01   Nicholas
                 59B02   Ellen

58B01 John Hampton
   Son of John Hampton (56M02)
           and Elizabeth Hasaldine (56M01)
   Baptised 14 January 1584/5
   Buried 4 May 1596

59B01 John Hampton
   Son of Robert (57M01) and Anne (57M01)
   Baptised 17 February 1592
   Buried 4 May 1596

59B02 John Hampton
Son of Hugh Hampton (56M02)
and Jaine Wetherington (56M01)
Baptised 22 June 1599
Buried - see 54D01 or 54D02

59B03 John Hampton
Son of John Hampton (57M01) and Amy Meridith (57M01)
Baptised 7 November 1591
Buried 4 May 1596†

59B04 John Hampton
Son of John Hampton (57M02)
and Margery Wethington (57M01)
Baptised 7 October 1593
John is possibly the twin brother of Margret (59B01)

59M05 John Hampton
Married Gracie (59M01)
Children:

61B01	Lawrence
61B01	Elizabeth

Jone

52D01 Jone Hampton
Widow of Daringhton (Dorrington)
Buried 22 February 1598/9

54M01 Jone Hampton
Wife of Henry Hampton (54M01)
Maiden name unknown
Children:

56B01	Ellen
56B01	Hughe
56B01	Allys
57B01	Jone

57B01 Jone Hampton
Daughter of Henry (54M01) and Jone (54M01)
Baptised 7 February 1570

Katherine

56B01 Katherine Hampton
   Daughter of John (53M01) and Margeret
   Baptised 1 January 1569
   Buried 2 January 1569

64M01 Katherin Hampton
   2nd wife of John Hampton (57M01)
   Born Katherin Harper
   Married (2) John Hampton 23 Sept. 1602
   Buried 9 December 1607

64B02 Katherne Hampton
   Daughter of William (62M01) and Anne (62M01)
   Baptised 26 November 1649

Lawrence

61B01 Lawrence Hampton
   Son of John (59M05) and Gracie (59M01)
   Baptised 3 October 1619

Margaret, Margeret

51D01 Margaret Hampton
   Widow
   Buried 8 October 1589

53M01 Margeret Hampton
   Born Margeret Cranadg
   Wife of John Hampton (53M01)
   Maried John 28 October 1556
   Children:
            55B01 Margeriet
            56B01 John
            56B01 Elnor
            56B01 Katherine
            57B01 Rondolphe
   Buried 17 April 1601

55B01 Margeriet Hampton
Daughter of John (53M01) and Margeret Cranadg (53M01)
Baptised 13 July 1557

58B01 Margaret Hampton
Daughter of Hugh Hampton (56M02)
and Jaine Wetherington (56M01)
Baptised 11 August 1588
Buried 27 February 1588/9

59B01 Margeret Hampton
Daughter of John Hampton (57M01 or 57M02)
Baptised 7 October 1593

She was baptized the same day as John (59B04), Son of John
Hampton (57M02) and Margery (53M01), but the register simply
states that Margret was the daughter of John Hampton and wife

Margerie Margery

53M01 Margerie   Hampton
Wife of Hughe Hampton (53M01)
Maiden name unknown
Children:
55B01 Francis

57M01 Margerie Hampton
Wife of John Hampton (57M02)
Born Margerie Wethington
Married John Hampton 20 November 1592
Children:
59B01   Margeret?
59B04   John
59B01   William
59B01   Raphe?

61M01 Margery Hampton
Wife of Richard Hampton (61M01)
Children:
63B01   Hugh

Mary

61M01   Mary Hampton
    2nd Wife of Thomas Hampton (60B01)
    Children:
          63B01 Thomas

62B01 Mary Hampton
    Daughter of Thomas (60B01) and Elizabeth Trym (60M01)
    Baptised 28 November 1624

Nicholas

59B01 Nicholas Hampton
    Also known as Nicalas
    Son of John (57M03) and Elizabeth (57M01)
    Baptised 13 December 1594

Randolph Rondolphe

57B01 Rondolphe Hampton
    Son of John Hampton (53M01) and Margeret Cranag (53M01)
    Baptised 23 October 1575

Raphe

59B01 Raphe Hampton
    Son of John Hampton (57M02)
          and Margery Wethington (57M01)
    Baptised 5 March 1597

Richard

59B01 Richard Hampton
    Son of Hugh Hampton (56M02)
          and Jaine Wetherington (56M01)
    Baptised 22 April 1593

61M01 Richard Hampton
    Married Margery (61M01)
    Children:
          63B01   Hugh

Robert

56B01 Robert Hampton
Son of William Hampton (53M01) and Ellen (53M01)
Baptised 13 March 1563
Married Amey Fox (56M01) 8 January 1589
Died 1601 at Wetherington
Buried 20 June 1601

57M01 Robert Hampton
Married Anne or Ane (57M01)
Children:

59B01	Thomas
59B01	John
59B01	An
59B01	Alls

Thomas

59B01 Thomas Hampton
Son of Robert (57M01) and Anne (57M01)
Baptised 21 November 1590
Buried 6 May 1595

60B01 Thomas Hampton
Son of Hugh Hampton (56M02)
    and Jaine Wetherington (56M01)
Baptised 21 April 1602
Married (1) Elizabeth Trym (60M01) 5 August 1621
Children:
        62B01 Mary
Married (2) Mary (61M01)
Children:
        63B01 Thomas

63B01 Thomas Hampton
Son of Thomas (60B01) and Mary (61M01)
Baptised 14 September 1631

William

53M01 William Hampton
Married Ellen Moss (53M01) 10 October 1556
Children:
    56B01 Robert

57M01 William Hampton
Married Frances Bryst (57M01) 6 May 1590
Died at Blower Dales, Blore
Buried 10 November 1622

59B01 William Hampton
Son of John (57M02) and Margery (57M01)
Baptised 6 November 1595

59M02 William Hampton
Married An Roe (59M02) of Mucklestone 2 August 1610

60B01 William Hampton
Son of Hugh Hampton 56M02
    and Jaine Wetherington (56M01)
Baptised 23 January 1605/6

62M01 William Hampton
Married Anne (62M01)
Children:
    64B02   Katherne

The Hampton Family in Shropshire

Adderley

Johann (John) HAMPTON and Ann ELLERTON were married on 29 August 1708.

Maria (Mary) HAMPTON of Morton Sey and Johann (John) AVERELL of Ashley were married in Adderley on 3 October 1713.

Thomas HAMPTON, a yeoman of Morton Sey and Sarah SWANWICK, spinster of Adderley, were married by licence at Adderley on 27 December 1782. The wedding was witnessed by John SHERWIN and John COATES

Sarah HAMPTON and John LOW were married on 7 May 1804 at Adderley. The wedding was witnessed by Martha WHITTINGHAM and Daniel ALLMAN.

Alberbury

No Hamptons recorded in this parish

Ashley - see Adderley

Berrington

Willielmus (William) HAMPTON was buried on 30 February 1628. This entry appears between January 17 and February 14 so is probably a transcription error - the correct date could have been Feb 3 or 13. Note also that New Year's Day that year was March 25.

Amy HAMPTON, a spinster, and Geo. GRIFFITHS, a carpenter from Pitchford Forge, were married by licence on 4 January 1786.

Claverley

Elnor HAMPTTON and Robert BRIDGINDE were married at Claverley on 25 May 1586.

Condover

Ann HAMPTON and Thos. LEECH were married at Condover on 28 January 1722.

Catherine, the daughter of John and Joyce HAMPTON from Cond, was buried on 29 September 1768.

John HAMPTON from Cond, was buried on 11 December 1768.

Joyse HAMPTON was buried on 19 January 1811 aged 82 years (born 1729)

Montford

No Hamptons recorded in this parish

Morton Sey - see Adderley

Stanton Lacy

No Hamptons recorded in this parish

Selattyn

No Hamptons recorded in this parish

Whittington

Margaret, daughter of Richard HAMPTON of Francton, was baptised at Whittington on 13 August 1640.

Banns for the wedding of Margaret HAMPTON of the parish of West Felton and John ROBERTS of the parish of Whittington were read on June 26, July 3 and July 10 1768.

The Grindley Family

of

North Shropshire

By

Nancy and Geoffrey Lindop

Adderley

1730 Aug. 22. The burial took place of Viscount Kilmorey who was of the Grimley family.

1778 Feb. 8. James Grindley, husbandman, & Elizabeth Cooper, spinster, were married : Witnessed by Thomas Brown.

Atcham

1686 Jan. 1 Elizabeth Grindley was married, the groom's name is torn from the register.

1689 Apr. 25. Mossenden Carter & Margret Grindley were married.

Berrington

1752 Dec. 6. John Roberts & Anne Grindle were married.

Clive

1768 Aug 19 Mary, wife (or widow) of Mr. Grinley was buried.

Edstaston

1809 Nov 5. Richard natural son of Hannah Grindley of Edstaston was baptised.

Habberley

1602 Jan. 25. Thomas Grinlye, of Worthen Parish was buried.

1613 Mar. 20 Jane Grinlye was buried

Hodnet

1709 June 16. Richard, son to John Grindly & Rose was baptised.

1709 Dec. 24. Phillip, son to John & Rose Grindley was buried

1710 Jan. 1. Elizabeth, daughter to John Grindly & Rose was baptised.

1712 Dec. 6. John, son of John & Rose Grindley was baptised.

1715 Aug. 4. Phillip, son of John & Rose Grindley was baptised.

1717 Dec. 31. Margarett, daughter to John & Rose Grindley was baptised.

1725 Apr. 10. Elizabeth, daughter of John & Rose Grindley was buried.

1734 Sep. 6.   Rose, wife of John Grindley was buried.

1739/40 Feb. 28.   Elizabeth, wife of John Grindley was buried.

1739/40 Feb. 28.   William, son of John Grindley was baptised.

1754 Dec. 28.   John Grindley of Wollerton was buried.

1754 Aug. 22.   John, son of Thomas & Elizabeth Grindley of Wollerton was baptised.

1755 Nov. 18.   Margt., daughter of Thos. & Elizabeth Grindley of Losford was baptised.

1757 Nov. 5.   Mary, daughter of Thomas & Elizabeth Grindley of Losford was baptised.

1761 Aug. 30.   Jane, daughter of Thomas & Elizabeth Grindley of Hodnet was baptised.

1763 May 11.   John, son of Thos. & Elizabeth Grindley of Hodnet was buried.

1771 Aug. 8.   Edward Bradshaw & Sarah Grindley were married. The wedding was witnessed by Bnj Forrester & Thomas Cartwright.

1777 July 6.   Anne, daughter of Margaret Grindley of Hodnet was baptised.

1790 Feb. 14.   Thomas Grindley of Hodnet was buried.

1795 Mar. 22.   Maria, daughter of Elisabeth Grinley of Hodnet was baptised.

1798 Nov. 7.   Elisabeth, daughter of Anne Grinley of Hodnet was baptised.

1799 June 9.   Elisabeth Grindley of Hodnet was buried.

1805 Feb. 21.   Thomas Haynes & Ann Grindley were married by George Allanson, (Rector). The wedding was witnessed by John Maddox & Joseph Hughes.

Kinnerley

1717/8 March   Ann, daughter of John Grindall of Edgerley was baptised sometime between 9th and 26th March.

1721 Nov 22,   John, son of John Grinley of Edgerley was baptised.

1724 Sept 11   Thomas, son of John Grinley of Edgerley was baptised.

1727 June 16   Susannah daughter of John Grinley de Edgerley was baptised.

1728 Aug 11   John Grinley de Edgerley was buried.

1798 Feb 18   Thomas, son of William Grinley and Anne
                (Formerley Jones), Measbrook Ucha, farmer, was
                baptised. He was born. Jan 24.
1800 Mar 9   John, son of William Grindley and Anne (Formerley
                Jones), Measbrook farmer was baptised. He was born.
                Feb 6.
1801 Aug 1   William, son of William Grindley and Anne
                (Formerley Jones), Measbrook Ucha, farmer, was
                baptised. He was born. May 21.
1804 July 22   Rebekah, daughter of William Grindley and Anne
                (Formerley Jones), Measbrook Ucha, farmer, was
                baptised. She was born. April 30.
1806 July 20   Ann, daughter of William Grindley and Anne
                (Formerley Jones), Measbrook ucha, farmer, was
                baptised. She was born. June 24.
1808 Dec 29   Joseph, son of William Grinley and Anne (Formerley
                Jones), Measbrook farmer, was baptised. He was
                born. Dec 4.
1811 Jan 4   Mary, daughter of William Grinley and Anne
                (Formerley Jones), was baptised. She was born.
                Decembe 1, 1810.

Moreton Say

1697 Apr. 6.   William Allen & Mary Grindley were married.
1701 Jan. 30. John Grindley, a wheelwright, of Woodlands
                township was buried.
1701 May 1.   Ellen, daughter of John & Ellen Grindley, wheelwright,
                of Woodsland township, was baptised.
1702 Feb. 26. John Hampton, yeoman, & Widow Grindley were
                married.
1707 Dec. 29. John Grindley, of Moreton, sojourner, & Rose
                Massey, of the parish of Hodnet were married.
1738 Mar. 25. John Grinley, of the parish of Hodnet was burried.
1752 July 6.   Benjamin Grindley & Ann Hill were married.

Myddle

1721/2 Jan 1   Joseph Grinley, said to be of Wrenbury, in County of
                Chester and Anne Nonely were married.
1723 Mar 31   John, son of Joseph Grinley and Anne was christened.

Newtown

1811 Apr 7   George, son of Hannah Grindley, Northwood, a base child was christened.

St Martin

1833 June 30.   John Grindley, of the parish of Whittington, and Elizabeth Lloyd were married by license.

Wem

1717/8 Mar 23   Elizabeth, daughter of Moses Grinley and Mary was baptised.

Westbury

1783 Dec. 26.   Edward Grinley, of the parish of St. Julian's, & Sarah Rider were married. The wedding was witnessed by Edw. Rider.

1796 Jan. 26.   William Grindley, batchelor of the parish of Kinnerley, & Ann Jones were married by special licence by David Williams,(Curate).

Worthen

1777 Mar. 27.   Anne, daughter of William & Anne Grindley was baptised.

1777 Nov. 25.   John Weeks & Alice Wright were married. The wedding was witnessed by William Grindley.

1778 May 28.   Joseph, son of William & Anne Grindleywas baptised.

1779 Oct. 7.   James, son of William & Anne Grindley was baptised.

1782 July 1.   Jonathan, son of Wm. & Anne Grindley was baptised.

1784 June 20.   Martha, daughter of William & Anne Grindley was baptised.

Wrockwardine

1771 Sept. 15.   John, son of John Grindley & Eleanor was baptised.

1812 Apr. 3.   Thomas Vickers & Martha Grindley were married.

Parish Registers researched but no members of the Grindley family found.

Alberbury
Albrighton nr Shrewsbury
Astley
Battlefield
Cardeston
Condover
Fitz
Great Ness
Grinshill
High Ercall
Knockin
Lee Brockhurst
Llanyblodwel
Llanymynech
Longdon upon Tern
Meole Brace
Montford
Moreton Corbet
Pontesbury
Ruyton of the Eleven Towns
Stapleton
Tibberton
Uffington
Uppington
Waters Upton
Weston under Redcastle
Whittington
Withington
Wroxeter

Bibliography

All the following published by the Shropshire Parish Register Society.

Parish	Publication	Coverage
Adderley	Lichfield Volume 4	Baptisms 1692-1812 Marriages 1692-1812 Burials 1692-1812
Alberbury	Hereford Volume 6	Baptisms 1564-1812 Marriages 1564-1812 Burials 1564-1779
Albrighton nr Shrewsbury	Lichfield Volume 1	Baptisms 1649-1812 Marriages 1649-1812 Burials 1649-1812
Astley	Lichfield Volume 4 part 1	Baptisms 1695-1815 Marriages 1754-1812 Burials 1695-1815
Atcham	Lichfield Vol 14 Part 2	Baptisms 1621-1812 Marriages 1621-1837 Burials 1621-1812
Battlefield	Lichfield Volume 1	Baptisms 1663-1812 Marriages 1663-1812 Burials 1663-1812
Berrington	Lichfield Volume 14 part 4	Baptisms 1560-1812 Marriages 1561-1837 Burials 1560-1812
Cardeston	Hereford Volume 5 Part 5	Baptisms 1678-1706 Marriages 1678-1706 Burials 1678-1706
Clive	Lichfield Volume 8 part 2	Baptisms 1676-1812 Marriages 1676-1812 Burials 1676-1812

Parish	Publication	Coverage
Condover	Lichfield Volume 6 Part 1	Baptisms 1570-1812 Marriages 1570-1812 Burials 1570-1812
Edstaston	Lichfield Volume 10	Baptisms 1713-1812 Marriages 1731-1753 Burials 1712-1812
Fitz	Lichfield Volume 4	Baptisms 1559-1812 Marriages 1559-1812 Burials 1559-1812
Great Ness	Lichfield Volume 20	Baptisms 1589-1864 Marriages 1589-1864 Burials 1589-1864
Grinshill	Lichfield Volume 2	Baptisms 1592-1812 Marriages 1592-1812 Burials 1592-1812
Habberley	Hereford Volume 5 Part 4	Baptisms 1598-1812 Marriages 1600-1822 Burials 1598-1812
High Ercall	Lichfield Volume 20 Part 3	Baptisms 1585-1651 Marriages 1585-1651 Burials 1585-1651
Hodnet	Lichfield Volume 11 Part 1	Baptisms 1540-1812 Marriages 1540-1812 Burials 1540-1812
Kinnerley	St. Asaph Volume 3	Baptisms 1661-1812 Marriages 1661-1812 Burials 1661-1812
Knockin	St. Asaph Volume 3	Baptisms 1673-1812 Marriages 1673-1812 Burials 1673-1812
Lee Brockhurst	Lichfield Vol 19 Part 4	Baptisms 1569-1838 Marriages 1569-1838 Burials 1569-1838

Parish	Publication	Coverage
Llanyblodwel	St. Asaph Volume 3	Baptisms 1599-1812 Marriages 1599-1812 Burials 1599-1812
Llanymynech	St Asaph Volume 8 Part 2	Baptisms 1666-1812 Marriages 1666-1812 Burials 1666-1812
Longdon upon Tern	Lichfield Volume 2	Baptisms 1692-1812 Marriages 1692-1812 Burials 1692-1812
Meole Brace	Hereford Vol 18 Parts 3 & 4	Baptisms 1681-1812 Marriages 1681-1837 Burials 1681-1812
Montford	Lichfield Volume 7 Part 1	Baptisms 1573-1812 Marriages 1573-1812 Burials 1573-1812
Moreton Corbet	Lichfield Volume 1	Baptisms 1580-1812 Marriages 1580-1812 Burials 1580-1812
Moreton Say	Lichfield Vol 8 Part 3	Baptisms 1691-1812 Marriages 1691-1812 Burials 1691-1812
Myddle	Lichfield Volume 19	Baptisms 1541-1810 Marriages 1541-1810 Burials 1541-1810
Newtown	Lichfield Volume 10	Baptisms 1779-1813 Burials 1740-1812
Pontesbury	Hereford Vol 12	Baptisms 1531-1812 Marriages 1531-1812 Burials 1531-1812

Parish	Publication	Coverage
Ruyton of the Eleven Towns	Lichfield Volume 5 Part 2	Baptisms 1719-1812 Marriages 1719-1812 Burials 1719-1812
St Martin	St Asaph Volume 8 parts 2, 3 & 4	Baptisms 1603-1812 Marriages 1603-1837 Burials 1603-1812
Stapleton	Lichfield Volume 1	Baptisms 1635-1812 Marriages 1635-1812 Burials 1635-1812
Tibberton	Lichfield Volume 13	Baptisms 1719-1812 Marriages 1719-1812 Burials 1719 -1812
Uffington	Lichfield Volume 5 Part 1	Baptisms 1578-1812 Marriages 1578-1812 Burials 1578-1812
Uppington	Lichfield Volume 2	Baptisms 1650-1812 Marriages 1650-1812 Burials 1650-1812
Waters Upton	Lichfield Volume 13	Baptisms 1547-1812 Marriages 1547-1812 Burials 1547-1812
Wem	Lichfield Vol 9 &10	Baptisms 1583-1812 Marriages 1582-1812 Burials 1582-1812
Westbury	Hereford Volume 12 Part 2	Baptisms 1538-1812 Marriages 1538-1812 Burials1538-1812
Weston under Redcastle	Lichfield Volume 11 Part 2	Baptisms 1565-1812 Marriages 1565-1812 Burials 1565-1812

Parish	Publication	Coverage
Whittington	St Asaph Vol 2 Part 2	Baptisms 1591-1812 Marriages 1591-1812 Burials 1591-1812
Withington	Lichfield Volume 5 Part 1	Baptisms 1592-1812 Marriages 1592-1812 Burials 1592-1812
Worthen	Hereford Volume 11	Baptisms 1558-1812 Marriages 1558-1812 Burials 1558-1812
Wrockwardine	Lichfield Vol 8 Part 3	Baptisms 1691-1812 Marriages 1691-1812 Burials 1691-1812
Wroxeter	Lichfield Volume 11	Baptisms 1613-1812 Marriages 1613-1812 Burials 1613-1812

Mercianotes specialises in the local history of places in
Cheshire, Shropshire and Staffordshire
and the genealogies of the people who lived there.
Especially the work of Nancy Lindop.
For details of other books in this series
and the rest of the Mercianotes range
please visit the website:

www.mercianotes.com

www.ingramcontent.com/pod-product-compliance
Lightning Source LLC
Chambersburg PA
CBHW071344290326
41933CB00040B/2331

www.ingramcontent.com/pod-product-compliance
Lightning Source LLC
Chambersburg PA
CBHW071344290326
41933CB00040B/2331